This journal belongs to:

____